SUPER
SANDCASTLE·
Let's Look A to Z

Appleseed
to
Zamboni

Famous Men from A to Z

Mary Elizabeth Salzmann

Consulting Editor, Diane Craig, M.A./Reading Specialist

ABDO
Publishing Company

Published by ABDO Publishing Company, 8000 West 78th Street, Edina, Minnesota 55439. Copyright © 2009 by Abdo Consulting Group, Inc. International copyrights reserved in all countries. No part of this book may be reproduced in any form without written permission from the publisher. Super SandCastle™ is a trademark and logo of ABDO Publishing Company.

Printed in the United States.

Editor: Pam Price
Content Developer: Nancy Tuminelly
Cover and Interior Design and Production: Colleen Dolphin, Mighty Media
Photo Credits: Corbis Images, Getty Images, English School/Getty Images, FPG/Getty Images, Giuseppe or Josef Grassi/Getty Images, MLB Photos/Getty Images, Michael Ochs Archives/Getty Images, After Gilbert Stuart/Getty Images, Time & Life Pictures/Getty Images, Shutterstock

Library of Congress Cataloging-in-Publication Data

Salzmann, Mary Elizabeth, 1968-

Appleseed to Zamboni : famous men from A to Z / Mary Elizabeth Salzmann.

   p. cm. -- (Let's look A to Z)

ISBN 978-1-60453-012-4

1. Celebrities--Anecdotes--Juvenile literature. 2. English language--Alphabet--Juvenile literature. I. Title.

CT107.S28 2008

920.02--dc22

[B]

2007050941

Super SandCastle™ books are created by a team of professional educators, reading specialists, and content developers around five essential components—phonemic awareness, phonics, vocabulary, text comprehension, and fluency—to assist young readers as they develop reading skills and strategies and increase their general knowledge. All books are written, reviewed, and leveled for guided reading, early reading intervention, and Accelerated Reader® programs for use in shared, guided, and independent reading and writing activities to support a balanced approach to literacy instruction.

About Super SandCastle™

Bigger Books for Emerging Readers
Grades K-4

Created for library, classroom, and at-home use, Super SandCastle™ books support and engage young readers as they develop and build literacy skills and will increase their general knowledge about the world around them. Super SandCastle™ books are part of SandCastle™, the leading preK–3 imprint for emerging and beginning readers. Super SandCastle™ features a larger trim size for more reading fun.

Let Us Know

Super SandCastle™ would like to hear your stories about reading this book. What was your favorite page? Was there something hard that you needed help with? Share the ups and downs of learning to read. We want to hear from you! Send us an e-mail.

sandcastle@abdopublishing.com

Contact us for a complete list of SandCastle™, Super SandCastle™, and other nonfiction and fiction titles from ABDO Publishing Company.

www.abdopublishing.com • 8000 West 78th Street Edina, MN 55439 • 800-800-1312 • 952-831-1632 fax

This fun and informative series employs illustrated definitions to introduce emerging readers to an alphabet of words in various topic areas. Each page combines words with corresponding images and descriptive sentences to encourage learning and knowledge retention. AlphagalorZ inspires young readers to find out more about the subjects that most interest them!

The "Guess what?" feature expands the reading and learning experience by offering additional information and fascinating facts about specific words or concepts. The "More Words" section provides additional related A to Z vocabulary words that develop and increase reading comprehension.

These books are appropriate for library, classroom, and home use.

Aa

Johnny Appleseed

1774-1845

Johnny Appleseed planted apple orchards throughout Ohio and Indiana.

He was also known for doing whatever he could to help other people and animals.

Guess what?

Johnny Appleseed rarely wore shoes, even in winter.

1847-1922

Alexander Graham Bell

Alexander Graham Bell was a scientist and an inventor.

He is most famous for inventing the telephone in 1875.

"Before anything else, preparation is the key to success."

Bb

1864-1943

George Washington Carver

George Washington Carver taught people how to be better farmers.

He showed farmers how planting different crops each year improves the health of plants.

He encouraged people to grow peanuts by creating a list of over 300 ways to use them.

Guess what?

George Washington Carver was the first African American student at Iowa State University.

Cc

"If you can dream it, you can do it."

1901–1966

Dd

Walt Disney

Walt Disney was a film director and an animator.

He created many famous cartoon characters, including Mickey Mouse.

Duke Ellington

Duke Ellington was a jazz composer and a band leader.

He played more than 20,000 concerts around the world and won 13 Grammy Awards.

Ee

"A problem is a chance for you to do your best."

1899–1974

Henry Ford

Henry Ford invented the Model T and started the Ford Motor Company.

His factories were the first to use assembly lines to speed up production.

1863–1947

Guess what?

In 1918, half of the cars in the United States were Model Ts.

Galileo Galilei

Gg

"We cannot teach people anything; we can only help them discover it within themselves."

Galileo Galilei was an Italian scientist and astronomer.

He made a better telescope that could be used to study the stars, planets, and moons.

He proved that the earth revolves around the sun.

1564–1642

1905–1976

Guess what?

Howard Hughes was one of the most famous people in the United States. But, he rarely went out in public during the last 25 years of his life.

Hh

Howard Hughes

Howard Hughes was a filmmaker, engineer, and pilot.

He built fast airplanes and set many flying records.

1783-1859

Washington Irving

Washington Irving was an American writer and diplomat.

Two of his best-known stories are "The Legend of Sleepy Hollow" and "Rip Van Winkle."

Guess what?

Washington Irving's parents named him after George Washington.

Ii

Thomas Jefferson

Thomas Jefferson was the second vice president and the third president of the United States.

He was also the main writer of the Declaration of Independence.

1743-1826

Jj

"Never put off till tomorrow what you can do today."

Kk

Martin Luther King Jr.

Martin Luther King Jr. was an American civil rights leader.

He is especially remembered for his famous "I have a dream" speech.

"Everybody can be great, because everybody can serve."

1929-1968

1809–1865

Abraham Lincoln

Abraham Lincoln was the sixteenth president of the United States.

He was president during the Civil War.

He led Congress to end slavery throughout the United States.

Guess what?

Abraham Lincoln's face is on Mount Rushmore and the U.S. penny.

Wolfgang Amadeus Mozart

Wolfgang Amadeus Mozart was a classical composer.

He wrote different kinds of music, including symphonies, operas, and chamber pieces.

1756-1791

Mm

Guess what?

Mozart wrote his first composition when he was five years old.

Isaac Newton

> "No great discovery was ever made without a bold guess."

Isaac Newton was an English scientist and mathematician.

An apple falling from a tree inspired him to figure out how the earth's gravity works.

Nn

1642–1727

"One chance is all you need."

1913-1980

Jesse Owens

Jesse Owens was a track-and-field star in running and long jump.

In the 1936 Olympic Games, he won four gold medals.

In college, he broke three world records.

1935–1977

Pp

Elvis Presley

Elvis Presley was a musician, singer, and actor.

He was known as the King of Rock 'n' Roll or the King.

Guess what.?

Elvis Presley's home is named Graceland and is a National Historic Landmark.

Qq

Anthony Quinn

1915–2001

Anthony Quinn was the first Mexican American actor to win an Academy Award.

He was also a painter and a sculptor and won art competitions before he started acting.

Guess what?

Anthony Quinn started sculpting when he was nine years old.

George Herman "Babe" Ruth

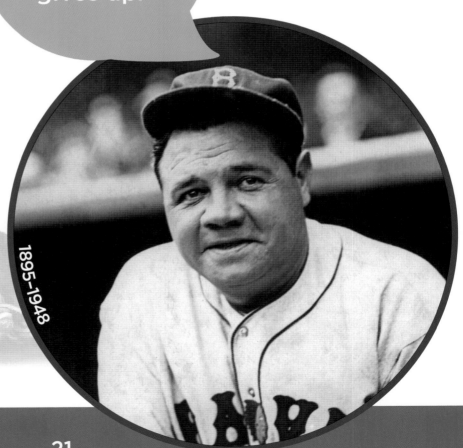

1895-1948

Babe Ruth was one of the best baseball players of all time.

He started out as a pitcher but later played first base and outfield.

Babe Ruth is best known for being a great batter.

Charles M. Schulz

Charles Schulz **was the cartoonist who created the** *Peanuts* **comic strip.**

Peanuts **characters include Charlie Brown, Snoopy, and Peppermint Patty.**

Charles Schulz **wrote** *Peanuts* **for almost fifty years.**

Ss

1922–2000

1888-1953

Jim Thorpe

Jim Thorpe was an American Indian athlete.

In the 1912 Olympic Games, he won two gold medals in track and field.

Later he played professional baseball and football.

"I have always liked sport and only played or run races for the fun of the thing."

Tt

Uu

"Comedy is simply a funny way of being serious."

1921–2004

Peter Ustinov

Peter Ustinov was an actor and a writer.

He was the voice of Prince John, the lion in Disney's *Robin Hood*.

1878–1923

Francisco "Pancho" Villa

Pancho Villa was a leader of the Mexican Revolution who became a Mexican folk hero.

He fought to free Mexico from dictator Porfirio Díaz.

Guess what?

Pancho Villa's real name was Doroteo Arango.

Vv

George Washington

1732-1799

George Washington was the first president of the United States.

Before he became president, he led the Americans in the Continental army during the Revolutionary War.

Ww

Guess what?

George Washington's face is on Mount Rushmore and the U.S. dollar bill.

Malcolm X

1925–1965

Malcolm X was a Muslim minister and civil rights leader.

He encouraged African Americans to fight for equality and justice.

"The future belongs to those who prepare for it today."

1865–1939

William Butler Yeats

"There are no strangers here; Only friends you haven't yet met."

William Butler Yeats was an Irish poet and playwright.

In 1923, he won the Nobel Prize in Literature.

Yy

Frank Zamboni

Frank Zamboni invented the Zamboni ice resurfacer in 1949.

Zambonis are used to smooth the surface of ice-skating rinks.

Guess what?

Before the Zamboni existed, it took several people longer than an hour to smooth an ice rink.

1901-1988

Glossary

animator – someone who makes the characters in a cartoon move in a lifelike way.

assembly line – a way of making something in which the item moves from worker to worker until it is finished.

astronomer – someone who studies objects and matter outside the earth's atmosphere, such as planets, moons, and stars.

athlete – someone who is good at sports or games that require strength, speed, or agility.

chamber – an enclosed space or section.

civil rights – the individual rights of a citizen, such as the rights to vote and to equality.

comic strip – a series of drawings that tell a story.

competition – a contest.

composition – an artistic work, such as a poem or a song.

dictator – a ruler with complete control who often governs in a cruel or unfair way.

diplomat – someone who works to help the governments of different countries get along.

engineer – someone who is trained to design and build structures such as machines, cars, or roads.

equality – the state of being the same.

filmmaker – someone who makes movies.

mathematician – a math expert.

orchard – a place where fruit or nut trees are grown.

pilot – a person who operates an aircraft or a ship.

professional – doing something for money rather than for pleasure.

revolve – to move in a circular path around something.

rink – an enclosed ice surface used for ice hockey or ice-skating.

sculpt – to create a three-dimensional work of art.

sculptor – someone who creates three-dimensional works of art.

symphony – a long musical composition that is played by an orchestra.

telescope – a magnifying device used to look at things that are far away.

More Famous Men!

Can you learn about these men too?

Aristotle	Mohandas Gandhi	George S. Patton
Louis Armstrong	Vincent van Gogh	Walter Payton
Arthur Ashe	Ulysses S. Grant	Pablo Picasso
Fred Astaire	Alexander Hamilton	Kirby Puckett
Johann Sebastian Bach	Harry Houdini	Ronald Reagan
J. M. Barrie	Langston Hughes	Paul Revere
César Chávez	Burl Ives	Jackie Robinson
Winston Churchill	Andrew Jackson	Franklin D. Roosevelt
William Clark	John F. Kennedy	John Philip Sousa
Buffalo Bill Cody	Francis Scott Key	Mark Twain
Christopher Columbus	Robert E. Lee	John Tyler
Charles Darwin	Leonardo da Vinci	Johnny Unitas
Joe DiMaggio	Meriwether Lewis	Frank Lloyd Wright
W. E. B. DuBois	Charles Lindbergh	Orville and Wilbur Wright
Thomas Edison	James Madison	Jack Butler Yeats
Albert Einstein	Thurgood Marshall	Ferdinand Zeppelin
Dwight D. Eisenhower	James Monroe	Florenz Ziegfield
Benjamin Franklin	Alfred Bernhard Nobel	Paul Zindel